DISNEY's
THE ARISTOCATS
and
Magical Me!

Place a
picture of
yourself here.

My name is:

I am [ ] years old.

I received this Disney Keepsake Classic from:

I started writing and drawing
my magical memories on:

Date

About Magical Me!

HERE IS A DRAWING OF ME...

...and 10 words that describe me!

A _____
R _____
I _____
S _____
T _____
O _____
C _____
A _____
T _____
S _____

DISNEY'S
THE ARISTOCATS

Magical Me!

Disney

KEEPSAKE CLASSIC

Magical Me!

DUCHESS LIVES WITH HER THREE KITTENS AND MADAME BONFAMILLE.

This is my Family.

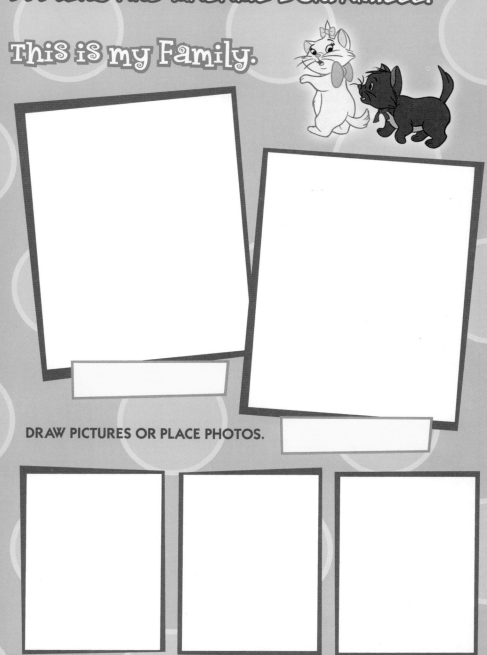

DRAW PICTURES OR PLACE PHOTOS.

Thomas O'Malley the Alley cat is a good friend to Duchess.

THESE ARE MY BEST FRIENDS. I'VE WRITTEN TWO WORDS THAT DESCRIBE EACH ONE!

_____ IS _____
(name)   AND _____.

_____ IS _____
(name)   AND _____.

_____ IS _____
(name)   AND _____.

Duchess and her family live in a big, beautiful house in Paris.

This is where I live.

These are some of the special things in my room.

Draw pictures or place photos.

imagine this...

If I had a big house in Paris,
I would have all these pets!

A DRAWING BY MAGICAL ME.

Toulouse is a talented artist.
Berlioz plays the piano.
Marie is a wonderful singer.

I AM TALENTED, TOO! I CAN:

1. _____

2. _____

3. _____

AND I WANT TO GROW UP TO BE THESE 5 THINGS:

1. _____

2. _____

3. _____

4. _____

5. _____

My Letter to...

Duchess, Marie, Toulouse, Berlioz, or O'Malley

Dear _____,

_____

_____

_____

_____

_____

_____

From your magical friend,

_____

The Magic Begins...

DISNEY

KEEPSAKE CLASSIC

The Magic Begins...

DISNEY'S
THE ARISTOCATS

Long ago, in the beautiful city of Paris, there lived a wealthy lady and her family of cats. There was Duchess, the mother cat, and her three darling (and sometimes mischievous) kittens, Toulouse, Marie, and Berlioz.

They lived in a mansion on an elegant, tree-lined street and were served the very best food on silver trays. They even slept in their own canopied bed in Madame's room.

These were no ordinary cats—they were *Aristocats*.

Madame Adelaide Bonfamille was a kind, gracious lady who loved sharing her beautiful home with Duchess and the kittens.

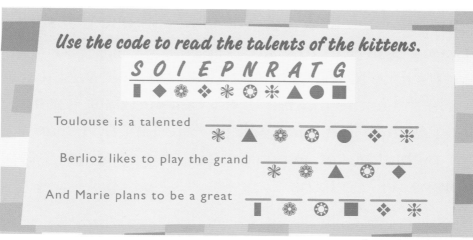

Use the code to read the talents of the kittens.

S	O	I	E	P	N	R	A	T	G
■	◆	❀	❖	✳	◉	✳	▲	●	■

Toulouse is a talented ✳ ▲ ❀ ◉ ● ❖ ✳

Berlioz likes to play the grand ✳ ❀ ▲ ◉ ◆

And Marie plans to be a great ■ ❀ ◉ ■ ❖ ✳

Madame loved her cats so much that she wanted to make sure they would enjoy the good life even after she was gone. So one day she asked her lawyer to visit.

"It's time to make my will," she said. "I wish to leave my entire fortune to my beloved cats. For as long as they live, they will be cared for by Edgar, my faithful butler. When the cats are gone, my fortune will go to him."

Downstairs, Edgar the butler was listening to every word through a pipe. He was angry that he would have to wait for the cats to die before he got any money.

Which line leads to each Aristocat?

A B C D

So Edgar decided to get rid of the cats as soon as he could. That evening, he sprinkled sleeping  pills in their milk.

"Cats first, and I come after the cats? That's not fair!" he muttered. "Those cats have to go so I can get the fortune first."

Edgar planned to wait until the cats were in a deep sleep and then sneak them out of the house in a basket and take them to the country.

"Here you are," said Edgar, setting down the bowls of milk. "My specialty–crème de la crème à la Edgar!"

The cats and their friend, Roquefort the mouse, lapped up every drop. The cats just managed to stagger to their basket before they fell into a deep sleep.

Match Roquefort to his shadow.

A   B   C

That night, when Madame was in bed, Edgar sneaked the cats out of the house. He climbed onto his motorbike thinking about how he would take Duchess and the kittens way out in the countryside and leave them!

But Edgar's plans were spoiled!

Just outside Paris, two dogs jumped out at the motorbike, barking and snarling, giving Edgar a terrible fright.

As he swerved, the basket of sleeping cats tumbled out of the sidecar, and Edgar sped off, leaving it behind. He just wanted to get home before the dogs attacked him.

These are 3 words that describe Edgar:

_____   _____   _____

The next morning, the cats crawled out of their basket and found themselves under a bridge by a river. They were scared and thought they had dreamed a bad dream.

"How did we get here?" asked Berlioz, looking around in confusion.

"*I* know—we were all riding and bouncing along, and Edgar was in the dream," said Toulouse. Then he had a thought. "It wasn't a dream. Edgar did this to us!"

"I don't know what happened, darlings," said Duchess, "but everything is going to be all right."

HELP duchess and the kittens find their way home to Madame.

départ

fin

As Duchess wondered what to do, an alley cat strolled by. He was singing, "I'm Abraham DeLacey... Giuseppe Casey... Thomas O'Malley the Alley Cat!" He gave a friendly smile when he saw Duchess and the kittens, and they smiled back at him.

When they told O'Malley they were lost, he offered to help them get back to Paris.

"Thank you," said Duchess, wiping away a tear with the end of her fluffy white tail. "You see, Madame loves us very much and she's all alone in that big house."

Duchess and the kittens followed their new
friend along a railway track that led all the way to
Paris. The kittens were racing ahead across the
bridge when suddenly they heard a train whistle
and *clickety-clack, clickety-clack, clickety-clack.*

"Careful, children!" Duchess warned.

But it was too late. The *whoosh* of a train
knocked Marie off the bridge and into the river far
below. Without a moment's hesitation, O'Malley
dived in after her.

WHICH MARIE IS DIFFERENT?

A

B

C

D

O'Malley rescued the terrified little kitten as
Duchess, Toulouse and Berlioz hung on for dear
life underneath the tracks.

"All right, now, don't panic!" O'Malley
ordered, as the train thundered on its way.

It was a narrow escape!

Let's Play!

Disney

KEEPSAKE CLASSIC

Let's Play!

TOULOUSE IS A TALENTED PAINTER. DRAW AND COLOR YOUR OWN AMAZING PICTURE.

WORD SEARCH

```
R D V Y L D E T N T W J H
T M U Q H I H O X J M M T
U K F C R M T U P Y B H Z
Y L J A H L Y L X K R O Q
P P M K J E W O H C I B R
L J A O K K S U Q L E V P
K H D P L M U S R B Z C K
J Y A H T J R E Z M Q H L
H B M B R Y B K M L S J G
G G E J A Z Z J N H I L J
F T L G G Y W R L G R P T
D V M S D J Y L I M A F D
S F N R E K S D P F P D C
```

Look up, down, across and diagonally for these words:

PARIS   **TOULOUSE**   **EDGAR**

MADAME   **BERLIOZ**   **FAMILY**

DUCHESS   **MARIE**   **JAZZ**

Marie's La Smoothies

Ask a grown-up to help you make this fun snack.

:3 You will need: 3:

1 small carton plain yogurt
1 cup orange, apple or white grape juice (to taste)
1 tablespoon honey
1 banana
Favorite fruit, like strawberries, blueberries or peaches
Crushed ice

Optional: ice cream, sherbet, or frozen fruit

:3 Directions: 3:

Rinse and slice fruit.

Place all ingredients into blender and spin until mixture becomes the crème de la crème of smoothies!

Pour into pretty glasses.

Makes about 3 servings.

DRAW THOMAS O'MALLEY THE ALLEY CAT!

Which Duchess is Different?

A

B

C

D

Ask family members and friends (and yourself!) to answer these fun questions. Write down their answers.

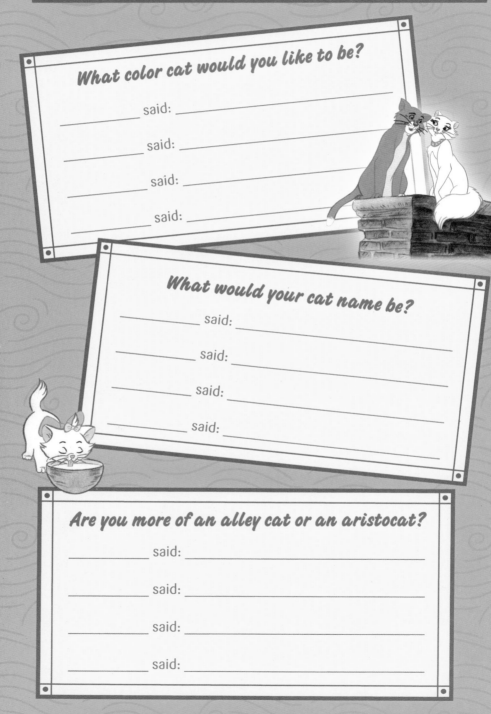

What color cat would you like to be?

_____ said: _____

_____ said: _____

_____ said: _____

_____ said: _____

What would your cat name be?

_____ said: _____

_____ said: _____

_____ said: _____

_____ said: _____

Are you more of an alley cat or an aristocat?

_____ said: _____

_____ said: _____

_____ said: _____

_____ said: _____

Which character are you most like from this story?

_____ said: _____

_____ said: _____

_____ said: _____

_____ said: _____

What instrument would you play in a cat jazz band?

_____ said: _____

_____ said: _____

_____ said: _____

_____ said: _____

HELP MARIE FIND HER WAY TO TOULOUSE AND BERLIOZ.

START

FINISH

The Magic Continues.

DISNEY

KEEPSAKE CLASSIC

The Magic Continues.

All that day and into the night, the little band of cats—Duchess, Marie, Toulouse, Berlioz and O'Malley—trudged on. Duchess and the kittens were used to riding in carriages, not walking along country roads and across rooftops!

By the time they reached Paris, they were exhausted.

"I'm tired, Mama," whined Marie.

"My feet hurt," said Berlioz.

"I bet we've walked a thousand miles," sighed Toulouse.

It was still a long way to Madame's mansion, so O'Malley invited Duchess and the kittens to stay at his house.

But when they got there, they found that O'Malley already had visitors. A group of alley cats, led by O'Malley's friend, Scat Cat, were playing jazz music.

The whole building was swinging to the beat!

CAN YOU FIND THE:

TRUMPET ☐

CYMBAL ☐

ACCORDION ☐

BASS ☐

GUITAR ☐

The kittens forgot about being tired and joined in the fun. Berlioz helped play the old piano, Toulouse kept time to the music, and Marie sang at the top of her voice.

Even Duchess couldn't resist joining in. She and O'Malley danced happily until midnight.

Paris is a fun city to visit – for a cat or a person.

A FUN CITY I TOOK A TRIP TO WAS:

_____

I WENT WITH: _____

WE GOT THERE BY TRAVELING IN A: _____

_____

SOME OF THE THINGS WE SAW THERE WERE:

_____

_____

TWO THINGS WE DID THERE:

1. _____

2. _____

(Draw picture or place photo here.)

I WOULD LOVE TO VISIT: _____

Later, after the jazz band left and the kittens were asleep, O'Malley and Duchess sat together in the moonlight, looking over the rooftops of Paris.

"I wish you didn't have to go," O'Malley said to Duchess. "And the kittens—they need a sort of… well… a father, don't they?"

Duchess wished she could stay, too. But she had to think of Madame.

"I'm sorry," she told O'Malley sadly. "We must go home tomorrow."

The next morning, as milk trucks rattled through the streets of Paris, O'Malley escorted Duchess and the kittens home to Madame's house.

The kittens scampered ahead and began to meow at the door of the mansion. Duchess and O'Malley stopped at the gate to say *au revoir*.

"Au revoir" is French for good-bye.

Can you match each French word to its English meaning?

CHAT	HELLO
CHIEN	NO
BONJOUR	BOY FRIEND
OUI	CAT
NON	GIRL FRIEND
AMIE	YES
AMI	DOG

Answers: chat-cat, chien-dog, bonjour-hello, oui-yes, non-no, amie-girl friend, ami-boy friend

What will Toulouse want to do when he's finally home again?.

Place sticker here.

"What a fancy neighborhood," O'Malley said a little sadly.

Duchess nodded. "I'll never forget you, Thomas O'Malley," she said fondly. "Thank you for bringing us home. Au revoir."

Then Duchess and her kittens hurried through their own little door into the house, eager to be back with their mistress, where they belonged.

Edgar was in the kitchen, celebrating with a bottle of champagne.

"Edgar, old chap, some day all this will be yours!" he said.

Then, suddenly, he heard the kittens.

"It can't be them!" he exclaimed. "It isn't fair!"

He ran upstairs to stop them before Madame realized they were back.

As the cats came through the door, a sack came down over their heads. Edgar took the sack out to the barn and put it in a *Place sticker to complete sentence.* that was being sent to Timbuktu.

"This time you'll never come back!" he said.

But Roquefort the mouse, who had come out to welcome the cats, saw everything. He dashed outside to tell O'Malley.

"Duchess and the kittens in trouble?" said O'Malley. "I'm on my way! But I'll need help. Get Scat Cat and the alley cats." And he told Roquefort how to find them.

Roquefort was scared of meeting these strange cats all by himself—but he would do anything to rescue his friends. He scurried off as quickly as he could.

At first the alley cats teased Roquefort and threatened to eat him, but at the mention of O'Malley's name they all agreed to help.

"Follow me!" the brave little mouse cried, as he led Scat Cat and the alley cats to Madame's house.

By the time Roquefort returned, Edgar had cornered O'Malley in the barn with a pitchfork. The alley cats stormed in, hissing, biting and scratching!

WHICH PIECE COMPLETES THE PICTURE?

A

B

C

YOUR ANSWER

While the alley cats dealt with Edgar,
Roquefort opened the lock on the trunk.
O'Malley helped Duchess and the kittens
out—and then the alley cats shoved Edgar
into that stuffy trunk and slammed and
locked the lid!

A few minutes later, who should arrive
but the deliverymen to pick up the trunk!

Edgar was on his way to Timbuktu!

Madame Bonfamille was thrilled to have
Duchess and the kittens back. She was also
delighted to meet O'Malley. "He's so
handsome," she whispered to Duchess.
"Let's ask him to join the family!"

Madame also decided to set up a home for all the homeless alley cats of Paris. From then on, all cats would be treated as special, wonderful *Aristocats*.

Add the sticker of ✳ Roquefort ✳ anywhere you want in this happy scene.

HOW MANY WORDS CAN YOU MAKE FROM THE LETTERS IN:

ARISTOCATS

_____   _____

_____   _____

_____   _____

_____   _____

_____   _____